Walks to
Teashops
Tale...
in Warwickshire

Richard Shurey

COUNTRYSIDE BOOKS
NEWBURY BERKSHIRE

First published 2003
© Richard Shurey 2003

COUNTRYSIDE BOOKS
3 Catherine Road
Newbury, Berkshire

To view our complete range of books,
please visit us at
www.countrysidebooks.co.uk

ISBN 1 85306 783 0

Designed by Graham Whiteman
Maps and photographs by the author
Cover design by Peter Davies, Nautilus Design

Produced through MRM Associates Ltd., Reading
Printed by Woolnough Bookbinding Ltd., Irthlingborough

Contents

Introduction   6

Walk

1 Kingsbury Water Park *(3½ miles)*   7
A delightful walk through a well-established water park,
with the opportunity to see plenty of wildlife.

2 Hartshill Hayes Country Park *(6 miles)*   12
Superb woodlands and a peaceful waterway to be
enjoyed on this circuit from Mancetter.

3 Knowle *(3½ miles)*   16
A level walk through gentle countryside and along the
Grand Union Canal.

4 Kingswood and Packwood House *(4½ miles)*   20
A visit to a great country house and an amble down an
impressive avenue.

5 Chadwick End and Baddesley Clinton *(5 miles)*   25
A lovely mixture of field paths, canal towpaths and
country lanes, with the chance to visit a fine National
Trust property.

6 Kenilworth *(4½ miles)*   30
A gentle stroll where the ruined castle at Kenilworth is
rarely out of view.

7 Church Lawford *(5 miles)*   34
A walk through a lonely landscape along the valley of the
Upper Avon.

8 Henley-in-Arden *(3½ miles)*   39
An energetic climb to The Mount, on which a castle was
once perched and then along undulating paths to
Preston Bagot.

9 Coughton Court and the River Arrow *(4½ miles)*   44
A delightful circuit that follows the meandering River
Arrow for part of the way.

10 Hatton *(5 miles)*   49
Something for everyone on this walk starting from Hatton
Country World and a chance to see the Hatton flight of
locks.

11 Ufton *(2½ miles)*   53
A pleasant stroll through a nature reserve to view the flora
and fauna.

12 Southam *(4½ miles)*   57
Starting from this historic town, the walk is over fairly level
ground and alongside the pretty River Itchen.

13 Alcester *(4 miles)*   62
Views galore on this route from the Roman town of
Alcester.

14 Wilmcote *(4 miles)*   66
A walk along the Stratford-upon-Avon Canal, with tea in the
village where Shakespeare's mother lived as a child.

15 Charlecote *(2½ miles)*   70
A magnificent Elizabethan house and a gentle valley saunter.

16 Wellesbourne *(4½ miles)*   74
A ramble through the Dene valley passing a lovingly-
restored watermill and a former stately home.

17 Bidford-on-Avon *(5 miles)*   78
A walk full of interest from this attractive riverside town,
once a haunt of the famous Bard.

18 Edge Hill and Upton House *(4 miles)*   83
A walk through beautiful woods overlooking the historic
Civil War battle site, with the opportunity to visit another
fine National Trust property.

19 Shipston-on-Stour and Barcheston *(2½ miles)*   88
A gentle stroll along the vale of the River Stour.

20 Shipston-on-Stour, Barcheston and Tidmington
(5 miles)   92
Another pleasant valley walk from this pretty country
town whose fine inns are a constant reminder of the
coaching era.

AREA MAP SHOWING LOCATIONS OF THE WALKS

① Kingsbury

Hartshill ② ● *Nuneaton*

● *Birmingham*

Knowle ③ *Coventry* ●   ⑦ Church Lawford
● *Rugby*

Kingswood ④   ⑥ Kenilworth
⑤ Baddesley

⑩ Hatton

⑧
Henley-in-Arden   ● *Warwick*

Coughton ⑨   Ufton ⑪   ⑫ Southam

Wilmcote
Alcester ⑬   ⑭   ⑮ Charlecote
⑯ Wellesbourne

Bidford-on-Avon ⑰   *Stratford-upon-Avon* ●

Edge Hill ⑱

⑲ Shipston-on-Stour
⑳

N

Introduction

This book combines walks in the delightful countryside of Shakespeare's Warwickshire, with some deserved refreshment before or afterwards in either a welcoming teashop or tavern.

There is an amazing assortment of these in the county. The old-fashioned inns still exist with basic traditional pub fare but others have been refurbished to provide a menu that makes eating out something really special. Teashops range from charming cottages to those that are part of a museum or country park. And most of the many National Trust properties in the county have tearooms although, squirrel-like, they tend to hibernate in the winter.

But whatever venue you choose, be it a pub or a tearoom, remember the verdict of the medical profession who emphasise the benefits of a country walk. It really is a wonderful tonic, alleviating stress and fostering good health. It is also a splendid family activity!

Perhaps the intellect is improved too – we read that all the great men of letters were avid walkers. Jonathan Swift was an early writer who showed the full appreciation of the moral and physical advantages of walking although without the proximity of teashops. It is said he spent much time in wayside inns to enjoy the talk of tramps and ostlers. Charles Wesley, too, in his early expeditions went on foot (sometimes twenty or thirty miles a day) not only to save horse hire but also to 'put spirit' into his sermons.

Shakespeare, besides being a sportsman, lawyer, theologian and so on, conscientiously observed his own maxim: 'Jog on, jog on, the footpath way' (*The Winter's Tale*).

The twenty walks in this book around the beautiful Warwickshire countryside are of modest length but, with the pub or teashop included, they will provide just as good an outing for the spirit.

All the routes are circular and easily undertaken. Parking suggestions are given – but please ask permission from pub and café proprietors before leaving your car in their car parks while you walk, and it goes without saying that you should also be a customer of course.

Happy teashop and tavern walking!

Richard Shurey

Walk 1
KINGSBURY WATER PARK

*A*mong *the joys of Kingsbury are the fine tracks and pathways for walkers. Our route follows clearly signed ways alongside large and small pools then takes us by the now sparky-clean River Tame. There is a short diversion to visit Kingsbury village with its cliff-top church, then we return to the start along the Woodland Walk – a lovely track between mature willows, many of which have fallen into adjoining marshland to provide interesting habitat for wildlife.*

 The Old Barn Coffee Shop at Kingsbury Water Park is, as its name suggests, in a redundant farm building. This place ('The Home of Milky Coffee') deserves to succeed with its enterprising approach – there are special events throughout the year with topics such as gardening, country crafts, art and sculpture. But it is the food that is the pièce de résistance – for example a choice of eight fillings for your jacket potato, the all-day Barn Door Breakfast and a wonderful array of cakes and pastries. Definitely a place to visit *after* your walk, not before! The shop is open every day from 10 am to 5 pm except Christmas Day. Telephone: 01827 874823 or visit the website to find out more (www. milkycoffee. co. uk).

Alternatively – or for mid-walk refreshment – there are inns just off the route at Kingsbury itself.

DISTANCE: 3½ miles.

MAP: OS Landranger 139 Birmingham and Wolverhampton.

STARTING POINT: Old Barn Coffee Shop and car park (GR 204959).

HOW TO GET THERE: Kingsbury Water Park is well signed off the A4097, a few miles east of Sutton Coldfield.

THE WALK

For much of the 20th century this area was hardly the ideal place for a country stroll. Here were vast noisy industrial machines as gravel was extensively worked. There were ugly pits and scars across the landscape. When the sand and gravel was exhausted, however, the County Council came up with a visionary scheme to turn the now water-filled pits and the surrounding 600 acres into a magnificent country park. The place was opened to visitors in 1975 and these days a great variety of leisure activities can be enjoyed.

1. In the top right corner of the car park walk along the nearby stony path. Go under high electricity wires. Follow the green arrowed way. At a junction of paths and a sign (Hemlingford and Centenary Way) bear right.

The Centenary Way is a long-distance recreational footpath established in 1989 to celebrate the 100th anniversary of Warwickshire County Council. It starts in the Water Park and ends 100 miles later at Meon Hill south of Stratford-upon-Avon.

2. Go over a footbridge by Hemlingford Pool. Walk beside the water. Follow the green arrows to walk through woodlands then across a vehicle way to border (to the left) a model boat pool.

To the right are woods planted in 1996 and maintained by the Beaver Section of the Mile Oak Sea Scout Troop.

3. Keep by the pool at a junction of tracks to go over a footbridge. Continue along the main pathway, so leaving the green arrowed way (which goes right). At a vehicle way cross to the opposite path (yellow arrow) to rejoin the vehicle way.

4. Turn left with Bodymoor Heath Water on the left and a smaller pool on the right. At a T-junction of vehicle ways turn left.

The ruins of Kingsbury Hall sit alongside the village church

You will notice traces of cat's-eyes along this track – this was once a main road until a new bypass was built. Now grass is creeping over the tarmac.

5. At a barrier before a bridge take the path over the grass to the left.

There are old arches on this bridge. This is the pensioned-off Hemlingford Bridge built by public subscription in 1783. Nearby is Kingsbury Mill which is crying out for rescue. A mill was recorded here in the Domesday Book of 1086 and rated at 9s 3d. The building has over the centuries been a gun-barrel mill, a paper mill, a leather mill and a grain mill.

6. The path follows the banks of Hemlingford Pool to a footbridge over the River Tame. You can cross the footbridge and steps to Kingsbury village, with its interesting church and old buildings and inns.

The root of the river's name is from an old word meaning 'dark river' and is common throughout the land with words such as the Teme, Thames and even Taff and Taf in Wales.
      The church is dedicated to St Peter and St Paul and dates from the 12th

century with the fine tower added two hundred years later. To the left of the church on a bluff above the river is a crumbling ruined mansion. This is Kingsbury Hall and with its history it is amazing that it is not being saved. It was here that the kings of Mercia had their palace, and a crumbling wall and arches indicate something of its old splendour.

7. Resuming the walk continue along the path with the river on the right side. The path goes under high power cables then gradually veers away from the river to cross a footbridge over a brook. Continue to the M42 motorway.

8. Do not go under the bridge but turn left. The wide track goes around bends to a junction of ways. Turn right then immediately left, signed as the Woodland Walk. Out of the woods the way divides by a 'pedestrians only' sign. Take the left hand fork to a tarmac way and keep the old direction. This leads to the car park and welcoming café.

Walk 2
HARTSHILL HAYES COUNTRY PARK

This varied circuit begins at the large village of Mancetter which is to the south-east of the town of Atherstone. From the inn we pass the 13th century Norman church, then continue along a lane to the Coventry Canal, where we follow the towpath for a mile or so. The canal is bordered by reeded banks where wildfowl scatter as we approach. Our path drops down a valley then rises to the glorious woodlands of Hartshill Hayes Country Park. Back on the lane the way twists and turns to a golf course. This upland course has wonderful views far over the valley and into Staffordshire before we join a lane to return to the pub.

 The Plough at Mancetter which dates from the 16th century is one of those rapidly disappearing plain country inns where there is good simple food, a warm welcome (especially for families), traditional pub games and nothing artificial. You can eat outside in the beer garden on a sunny day. The menu is of the 'with chips' variety. We know a salad is better for the diet-conscious but can we resist? In addition there are filled potatoes and a wide range of sandwiches but the winter specials are chips with the steaks. The beers include Greene King, Abbot, Marston's and Bass but many ramblers love the scrumpy cider. The opening hours are the standard pub times, lunchtime, evenings and Sundays. Telephone: 01827 716031.

DISTANCE: 6 miles.
MAP: OS Landranger 140 Leicester, Coventry and Rugby.
STARTING POINT: The Plough Inn car park, (GR 320967).
HOW TO GET THERE: Mancetter is on the B4111 just off the A5 near Atherstone. You can park at the inn (customers) or alongside the nearby green.

THE WALK

1. From the inn car park turn right to pass the church.

St Peter's church is from the 13th century with bells that have been ringing the Christian message for 600 years. The place is probably on the site of an earlier wooden church built as early as AD 930.

2. Within a few steps bear right off the main road to walk along a lane. Immediately before the canal bridge drop down the bank left to gain the towpath. Turn left and continue with the water on your right side. Stay by the waterway for about 1¼ miles.

The Coventry Canal is 38 miles long with 13 locks and was opened for traffic in 1790. It runs from Fradley to Hawkesbury and is popular for leisure boating as it connects several other canals such as the Oxford and Trent and Mersey.

3. At a road bridge gain the road and cross the water. On the left is a very attractive canal workshop and repair yard. Note the fine fish weathervane on top of the clock tower. Climb the road to Hartshill Green where there is another pub.

On the green is the bus shelter. It is a memorial to the celebrated Warwickshire poet Michael Drayton who was born nearby in 1563. The stone building was opened by John Betjeman.

13

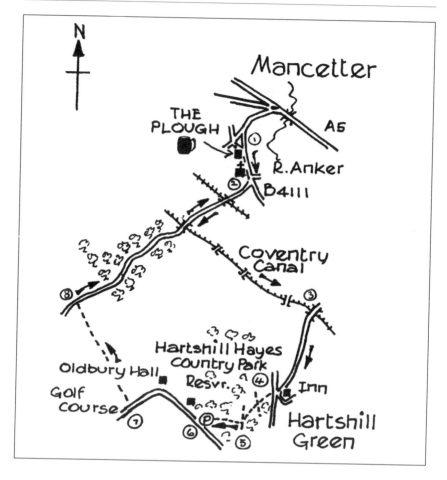

4. On the other side of the road take a footpath that is at the right hand side of the modern flats called Drayton Court. Walk by garages and pass through a wooden barrier. Drop down steps to cross boggy land along a raised causeway. Climb into the woods of the country park and keep ahead.

The woods of Hartshill Hayes Country Park were once part of the vast Forest of Arden. Towards the end of the 18th century there was much replanting of lime trees which provided blocks for the hat making industry of Atherstone. More recently beech and oak have been coppiced for timber for fences and thatching spars.

Hartshill boatyard on the Coventry Canal

5. At a crossroads of tracks keep ahead and maintain the heading to go over a railed bridge across a brook. Climb to a bold T-junction by a post numbered 3. Go left for 20 yards then right to regain the old direction. Now climbing along a twisting track keep ahead at another crossroads of paths by post 2 to reach a car park. (There are toilets here.)

6. Continue to a lane and turn right.

On the right is a large covered reservoir. The water provides a supply for Nuneaton. A little further on is the new Oldbury Hall. The former old building was destroyed by stray bombs in World War II.

7. After about ½ mile of lane walking go right along a signed path through a new metal gate. Follow the well-waymarked route over a golf course. Out of the course keep ahead over farmland to emerge on a lane.

8. Turn right to Mancetter and the Plough.

Walk 3
KNOWLE

*K*nowle *is an attractive village perched on the edge of the West Midlands conurbation and nudges some fine countryside. The High Street's old buildings are a constant reminder of past days. We leave the village to follow a stretch of towpath rambling alongside the wide Grand Union Canal. Quiet byways lead to some pleasant fieldpaths and past a sad ruined barn that for years has cried out for rescue. The route again meets up with the waterway and there are pathways back to the High Street and the goodies on offer at the teashop.*

The Mad Hatter's Café in Knowle has a tiny frontage – and indeed a small dining area – but it obviously is a very well known and popular eating place. The clientèle is mixed – shoppers wanting to rest weary legs, office and shop workers, businessmen and even walkers as the countryside can be reached in a few steps. The early customers love the breakfast sandwiches – toasted bread filled with bacon, egg, sausage and tomato; there is a choice of 20 sandwiches and the 'with chips' platters have ten varieties. All the food served is cooked to order so this is a place to relax awhile. Teas offered include Earl Grey and Fruit Tea – and the place is also licensed. The café is open daily Monday to Saturday from 8.30 am to 5 pm. Telephone: 01564 779806.

There are several inns nearby: the Red Lion, the Greswolde Arms and the Toby Carvery are all in the High Street. The latter two are open all day, every day.

DISTANCE: 3½ miles.
MAP: OS Landranger 139 Birmingham and Wolverhampton.
STARTING POINT: The fee-paying car park off the High Street almost opposite the café (GR 181769).
HOW TO GET THERE: Knowle is on the A4141 from Solihull. The Mad Hatter's Café is on the west side of the High Street.

THE WALK

1. Out of the car park turn right to the High Street. Turn left to pass Chester House.

Chester House houses the village library. It is timber-framed and dates from the 15th century. Behind the building is an award-winning knot garden that can be viewed from a raised platform.

2. At a junction by the church and Guild House bear left along the B4101.

The early 15th century church has a long dedication – to St John the Baptist, St Lawrence and St Anne. There is a spacious screen that was carved over four hundred years ago. The altar is Elizabethan. The Guild House was originally built in 1412 for the Guild of St Anne, a religious charity of the time. It was a shop until the early 20th century when it was restored.

3. Go past a junction then turn down Kixley Lane on the left. Walk to the end where there is a canal bridge.

4. Gain the towpath and continue with the water on your right side.

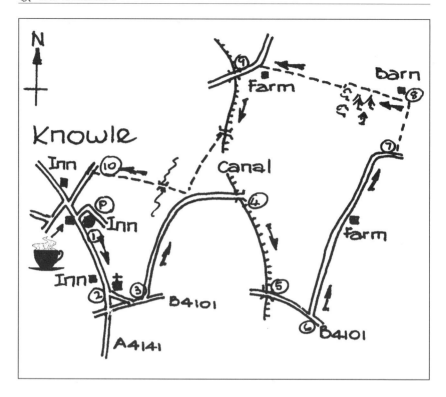

The Grand Union Canal is a pleasant escape route from the towns and cities of the Midlands. It was originally the Birmingham and Warwick Canal and was opened in 1842. It is little used now by commerce but is very popular with inland waterways enthusiasts.

5. At the next road bridge (bearing a notice 'Dead Slow passed (!) moored boats') leave the canal. Go up the bank to the road. Cross and turn right along the footpath.

6. Within 400 yards turn left along Elvers Green Road. Ignore one signed path on the left. After about ½ mile of lane walking take a signed footpath over a stile by a metal gate on the left.

7. Walk away from the lane over the open field. The path goes alongside a left hand wood. Follow the border of the field to go under power lines.

The church peeping through the trees to the right is at Barston. It is rather unusual for places of worship in this area as it is made of brick rather than stone. St Swithin's was built in 1721.

8. At a waymark (on an old gatepost) turn left to pass an ancient ruined barn that still retains rather nice brickwork. Walk alongside a left hand wood. When this ends turn left then at once right to regain the old heading. Follow the tractor way to a farmstead. Keep ahead along the drive and continue to a road. Turn left.

9. At a canal bridge gain the towpath. Walk with the water on your right to cross at a footbridge. Leave the canal along a clear path at the borders of fields. At a step stile two paths are signed. Take the right hand path and cross a footbridge. Continue along a clear path to a road.

10. Turn left to the High Street and cross. The café and car park are to the left.

The ruined barn passed on the walk

Walk 4
KINGSWOOD AND PACKWOOD HOUSE

This walk is a delicious amalgam of lanes, canalside towpaths and footpaths. After lane walking, the route is beside a straight section of the Grand Union Canal. Just beyond a road bridge there is a short connecting waterway to join another canal – the picturesque and narrow Stratford-upon-Avon Canal. This is always a 'must' for pleasure boat captains and crews but the section is hardly a holiday for them – the long Lapworth Flight takes the craft from the lowlands to the high Birmingham Plateau by many locks. We walk near Packwood House (National Trust) then along a fine avenue of mature trees, almost a mile long and through pastures where sheep graze, before a lane takes us back to the start.

 The delightful Punchbowl Inn in Mill Lane, Lapworth is not far from Packwood House. Inside it gives the illusion of being very 'olde-worlde' but in fact it was only built recently when it replaced a much older pub. There are stone-flagged floors and ancient beams incorporated in the structure and we are invited to 'rediscover the country pub'. A very good variety of beers are served, among them Bank's Best Bitter and Marston's Pedigree. The menu is not extensive but offers enough to satisfy all tastes, including vegetarian dishes. I can vouch for the mustard-glazed chicken as well as the glazed field mushroom dish topped with Stilton cheese. The pub is open daily from 12 noon to 11 pm (10.30 pm on Sundays). Telephone: 01564 784564.

There is a tea kiosk in the car park of Packwood House, open with the house from April to October.

DISTANCE: 4½ miles.
MAP: OS Landranger 139 Birmingham and Wolverhampton.
STARTING POINT: The car park of the Punchbowl Inn (GR 184720).
HOW TO GET THERE: From the A3400 at Hockley Heath follow the B4439 eastwards. Within 2 miles take a lane left (signed to Packwood House) which leads to the Punchbowl Inn.

THE WALK

1. Out of the car park go over the crossroads. Within ⅓ mile take a footpath signed on the right down the drive of Uplands Farm. At a barn turn right (with the barn now on your left). Keep ahead through rough land then over a vehicle drive. Walk to the end of a field. Through kissing gates follow the path to a road. Turn left and continue to a canal bridge. Gain the towpath and turn right, keeping the water on your left side.

The Grand Union Canal was the motorway of its age between London and Birmingham. It is almost 140 miles long and was formed by the amalgamation of many small waterways. The canal is almost 200 years old but when trade declined in the 1930s a vast scheme to widen it received Government support.

2. Go under the B4439 at Kingswood. About 400 yards further go over the footbridge. Turn right along the connecting canal. Go under a railway bridge to the junction of canals (Stratford is signed to the left and Kings Norton to the right). Go over the canal bridge.

Note the split down the middle of the bridge. This type of cast iron bridge allowed the horse and barge to stay as one without unhitching.

21

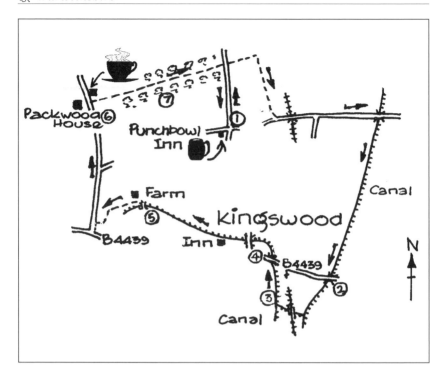

3. Continue along the towpath alongside large canal pools.

The Stratford-upon-Avon Canal was opened as a whole in 1816 mainly to convey coal south and limestone north. It was derelict for many years and almost officially abandoned in 1958. Canal enthusiasts saved it and in 1960 the National Trust took it over. Restoration work was undertaken by volunteer labour (including prisoners). It was reopened by the late Queen Mother in 1964.

4. Go under two road bridges. The towpath goes over a bridge then continues alongside the Lapworth flight of locks. There is a shop and inn nearby on the other bank.

5. At a lock cottage leave the canal. Go right along a vehicle way then turn left by a farm conversion. At a lane turn right to Packwood House.

6. Near stables (with fine sundials) and opposite the entrance to

The 16th century Packwood House

Packwood House turn right over the grass to climb steps and pass through a little metal gate. There is a good view of the house from here.

Packwood House originates from the 16th century but incorporates much from rebuilding in the 20th century. There is a good collection of old textiles and furniture. There is 300-year-old work from the celebrated pioneer of English tapestry, William Sheldon of Barcheston, South Warwickshire. The gardens of Packwood House are famous for the many topiary bushes which depict The Sermon on the Mount. Telephone: 01564 783294.

7. Walk through the pastures between the avenue trees. Climb a far stile by pools. Over stiles resume the avenue walk to a stile to a lane. Turn right to retrace your steps to the Punchbowl Inn.

Walk 5
CHADWICK END AND BADDESLEY CLINTON

There are no hills on this walk which is full of variety including a visit to a historic manor house. It starts with a stroll through the parkland of Baddesley Clinton Hall followed by a canalside path for a mile. The return leg is along delightful lanes and a fine bridleway over an open and lovely landscape to the churchyard of St Michael's church (beautiful with daffodils in springtime) and the secluded hall.

 The Orange Tree at Chadwick End is a rather special tavern. Dating from the 17th century, it has been skillfully modernised and the garden, with its pagodas and roses would not look out of place in a country house setting. It is just the place to relax after your ramble through the Warwickshire countryside. There is a fine selection of sandwiches available, if it is just a quick bite you are looking for, and the soup is excellent. However, this is a tavern where you can dine in style so why not stay awhile and sample the good food and wine on offer. The Orange Tree is open from 12 noon to 2.30 pm and 5.30 pm to 11 pm. Telephone: 01564 782458.

If you prefer afternoon refreshment, there is a tea-room at Baddesley Clinton Hall when this National Trust property is open (March to October).

DISTANCE: 5 miles.

MAP: OS Landranger 139 Birmingham and Wolverhampton.

STARTING POINT: The inn car park for patrons (GR 206731). Please notify the landlord that you are leaving your car while you walk.

HOW TO GET THERE: The Orange Tree is at Chadwick End, midway between Warwick and Solihull on the A4141.

THE WALK

If your walk is at the time of year when it is open, do visit Baddesley Clinton Hall (telephone: 01564 783294). The guidebook describes it as 'a romantic and atmospheric moated manor house, dating from the 15th century and little changed since 1634'. This was a refuge for persecuted Catholics and to date three priest's holes have been discovered. Keep looking – there may well be more in this intriguing house!

1. From the pub turn right along the main road. Within a few steps take a signed path over a stile on the right. Follow the direction indicated. The path (part of the waymarked Heart of England Way) follows a constant heading at the borders of fields then along a vehicle drive to a lane.

2. Turn right then left at a road junction. Within 50 yards take a signed path on the right. This is still the Heart of England Way so follow the waymarked route to a vehicle drive (leading to Baddesley Clinton Hall). Cross to the opposite stile.

3. Follow the arrowed direction to the far left hand corner of the field with the hall away to the left. Climb a stile and cross a brook. The path is now beside left hand woods. Over a stile to a large field bear right towards a brick barn. Climb a stile to the left of the barn and continue along a vehicle way to a road.

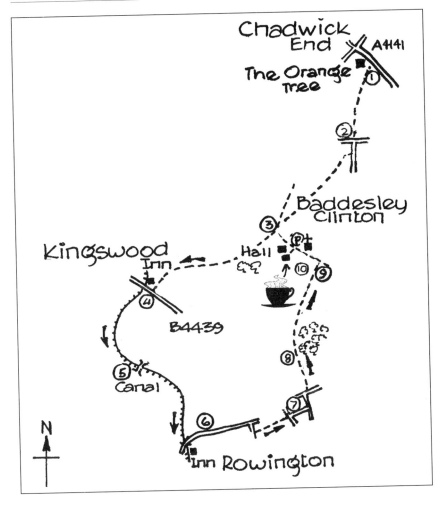

4. Turn right to pass an inn and come to a canal bridge. Gain the towpath and continue with the water on your left side. Go over the bridge across a feeder canal and keep along the towpath.

The waterway is the Grand Union Canal – in its day the 'motorway' to Birmingham. It was started in 1805 as the Grand Junction Canal from Braunston to connect with the Thames at Brentford west of London. There are about 100 locks on this section. It was always a busy route in the Canal Age and indeed is a popular route for pleasure cruising today.

Baddesley Clinton Hall is a fine moated manor house

5. Pass under a farm bridge and remain by the canal until bridge number 63. Go under this bridge and then up the slope to the right to the lane and turn right again to cross the water. On the right is another inn (open all day), if you are tempted to take a rest.

The Tom o' the Wood Inn was named after a local character called Tom who owned the sawmill at the nearby hamlet of Finwood.

6. Follow the lane to a road junction. Turn right. Within 300 yards take a path through a kissing gate on the left. The fenced path leads to a pasture. Keep ahead at the sides of fields to a stile to a lane.

7. Cross to the lane (The Avenue) opposite. At a T-junction turn left to another junction. Turn right. Immediately take a signed path through a metal gate left.

We are again on the Heart of England Way. This runs for about 100 miles from Cannock Chase in the north then to the east of Birmingham to join the Oxfordshire Way at Bourton-on-the-Water in distant Gloucestershire.

8. Keep ahead along a wide tractor way and pass through gates. At a multitude of gateways follow the arrowed way ahead. As the tractor way turns 90 degrees left maintain the old direction through a hunting gate. Continue at the side of an arable field. Go through a metal hunting gate and keep ahead to cross a brook. There is soon another hunting gate then a fenced way to a vehicle drive.

9. Turn left through a gate and walk through the churchyard of Baddesley Clinton church.

The 15th century St Michael's church has a tower built about 1500 by Nicholas Brome in remorse for having killed a priest. The tower has a turret stairway and eight gargoyles. There are memorials to members of the Ferrers family who lived at the Hall.

10. Keep the church on your right. Through a latch gate walk along a gravel path beneath sweet chestnut trees. Join the vehicle drive to the place where the drive was crossed earlier on the walk. Turn right and retrace your steps to the A4141 and the Orange Tree.

Walk 6
KENILWORTH

*F*or many years the pathways around Kenilworth have been a delight to encounter as there is a diligent footpath organisation that liaises with landowners and keeps stiles and bridges in good order. This walk starts along the track below the sturdy walls of the castle, giving us an unusual and spectacular view of the vast fortification. The route is then over fields to a quiet lane, little used as it only leads to farmsteads. The return leg borders an area where a celebrated steeplechase was run many years ago. A path crosses the site of Henry VIII's summer palace called The Pleasance. Little remains to show the former splendour – just hollows and hummocks.

Time for Tea, which is just off Castle Green in Kenilworth, is one of those old-fashioned family-run tearooms that you thought had long disappeared from the country scene. There are cheery staff who will brighten even the greyest of days, and you may be lucky enough to find the window seat free so that you can sit and watch the world pass by. In addition to the various teas offered there are seven types of coffee available. Time for Tea serves delicious light snacks and scrumptious cakes that are all home-made on the premises. It is open every day from 10.30 am to 5 pm except Mondays. Telephone: 01926 512675.

When the tearoom is closed you can make use of the Clarendon Arms next door. Telephone: 01926 852017.

DISTANCE: 4½ miles.
MAP: OS Landranger 140 Leicester, Coventry and Rugby.
STARTING POINT: The free car park of Kenilworth Castle (GR 280720).
HOW TO GET THERE: South-west of Coventry, Kenilworth Castle is well signposted off the B4103.

THE WALK

A tour of the castle either before or after the walk and teashop visit is a 'must'. The origins of the castle date from 1086 when Henry I gave the rocky knoll to his treasurer, Geoffrey de Clinton. Subsequently Henry II took over and increased the fortification. Later monarchs and dukes added their buildings too. In 1248 Simon de Montfort was in residence and made the place his headquarters for the Barons' Revolt. This resulted in the great siege of 1266.

1. Walk along the wide causeway from the car park towards the castle entrance. Just before railings and a gate drop down steps to the left and go through a kissing gate. Follow the track below the castle walls.

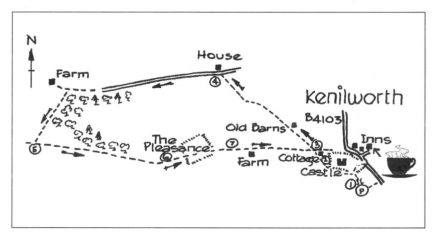

Kenilworth Castle

The reeded area to the left was once covered in a great pool so until the 17th century Kenilworth was an island fortress guarded by a 150 acre artificial lake. It was drained in 1650 by Colonel Hawkesworth, a Parliamentary officer who had 'slighted' (partially destroyed) the castle.

2. When the path splits take a left hand path to pass through a gate to the left of a thatched cottage. Turn left on Purlieu Lane to cross a brook.

This is Finehan Brook. Together with Inchford Brook it was dammed to form the castle pool, which was to play a large part in sustaining the six-month siege in 1266 until famine and disease forced the castle to surrender.

3. A few steps beyond the brook climb a stile on the right. Follow the path over the open field to pass by ruined barns. Keep on the same heading along clear paths through fields to emerge on a farm lane by brick-red cottages.

4. Turn left and follow the lane alongside woods. At the end and before a farm turn left, (with woods on the left), to drop downhill.

On a distant horizon you can just see a church. This is St John's at Honiley which takes its name from a historic well thought to have healing powers. Some say that the church was designed by Sir Christopher Wren who had retired to live at Wroxall Abbey a few miles away.

5. At a T-junction of tracks turn left. Walk at the edge of the field. Now a series of stiles and waymarks show the way, with Chase Wood on the the left.

6. We follow the track over the site of The Pleasance.

The Pleasance was a pavilion or summer lodge that was approached by barge along a channel from the great pool. It was the work of Henry V and was loved by subsequent monarchs. However, it was demolished by Henry VIII who then rebuilt it within the castle grounds.

7. Maintain the general direction to take a path on the left of a farm. The path leads to Purlieu Lane, which you follow to the thatched cottage. Pass through the gate and retrace your steps to the car park. The tearoom is on the left along the B4103 by Castle Green.

Walk 7
CHURCH LAWFORD

*T*he walk follows a pretty, scenic route along the valley of the Upper Avon. The river can be very fast-flowing and in days past the water powered many mills, the evidence of which we can see today. The industrial debris of wheels and machinery at Newnham Mill is passed early on the walk. There is an attractive stretch of lane walking to Little Lawford, where you will encounter some gems – the old hall and a restored mill with the water still rushing underneath. From here a bridleway goes over rather isolated countryside to Long Lawford which has an interesting 19th century church. The return for that well-deserved cup of tea is along pathways that hug the banks of the Avon.

The teashop (actually called a coffee shop here!) is in the Wyevale Garden Centre at Church Lawford. It occupies a corner that (with the roof lights) is lovely and bright even on the cloudiest of days. There are attractive table decorations and interesting framed prints of country scenes for sale. Various light snacks – sandwiches, pasties and rolls, that kind of thing – are available, all tastefully presented. There are cream cakes too, for those who just cannot resist. The tea/coffee shop which is run independently of the garden centre is open daily from 10.30 am to 4.30 pm.

The Old Smithy inn is nearby, in the centre of the village. Telephone: 01203 542333.

DISTANCE: 5 miles.

MAP: OS Landranger 140 Leicester, Coventry and Rugby.

STARTING POINT: The Wyevale Garden Centre car park (GR 449768). Alternatively, you could park on the street near the Old Smithy inn and start the walk by turning right down Smithy Lane.

HOW TO GET THERE: Church Lawford is just off the A428 midway between Coventry and Rugby. The Old Smithy inn is passed on the right. The Wyevale Garden Centre is well signposted and is at the bottom (north) end of the village.

THE WALK

As Church Lawford was recorded (as Leileford) in the Domesday Book of 1086 it is not surprising that there are many interesting old buildings including Manor Farm and the Old Rectory.

1. Out of the car park turn right along the main street of Church Lawford. Turn left down Smithy Lane.

As its name implies the village blacksmith's forge was here. It is still recalled by more senior residents as a place to gather and chat.

2. At the end of the lane go through a gate and keep ahead. Within 100 yards there is a crossroads of paths. Turn left. Walk through the fields with waymarks to show the way to the railed bridge across the River Avon. Go by the mill site and bear right up the slope to a stile. Two paths are signed; keep ahead, still climbing.

Glance left; in a farmyard is an isolated tower. This was once part of St Lawrence's church, built by the monks of Kenilworth Abbey. By 1794 the nave and chancel were demolished and in 1900 it was recorded the tower was without a roof. It was repaired by the Duke of Buccleuch and is now a protected

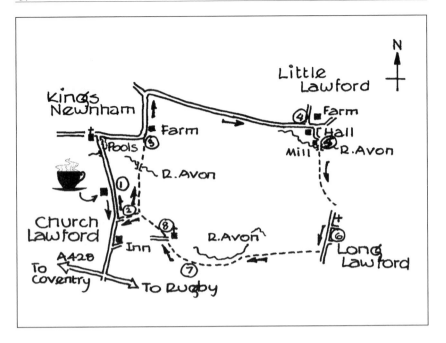

listed building. Nearby are three popular fishing pools that were made by the monks to store their fish for their Friday meals.

3. Pass through a gate and keep ahead to join a lane by houses. Maintain the direction. At a junction bear right – the lane is signed to Little Lawford.

Somewhere along this lane were the saline springs of Newnham Regis (the royal connection is that the land was owned by the monarch). It was hoped that the springs would rival those of Leamington Spa but the plans came to naught although the chronicler Ireland reported in 1795 that the springs were 'much frequented'.

4. Just past a junction after a mile and opposite a farm, turn right down a lane signed as a no through road. Pass the rather noble Little Lawford Hall.

What we see are actually the stables of the hall that are dated 1604. The great house was pulled down about 1790.

5. Just before the ford go left to pass in front of Little Lawford Mill. Keep on the bridleway that swings right around the mill. Pass through a gate and keep ahead to cross the river. Follow the wide way to pass through a gate to a lane by houses at Long Lawford. Keep ahead to pass a church.

St John's church without any spire or tower is only from 1839 but is admired because of the rare survival of its complete inside furnishings of the period.

6. Keep ahead along the road. By house number 19 turn right along a signed path. Go over a stile and continue to a meadow; walk alongside a right hand hedge. Go over a brook and keep ahead. Pass through a gate (waymark) and climb the rise. At the top go over a stile and take the direction indicated across the open field, now gradually nearing a railway.

7. Climb a stile then at once another. Turn right (right hand hedge). Go over a stile tucked in a far corner with the Avon to the right. Cross a

The tower is all that remains of St Lawrence's church

brook and go up steps. In the field follow a way near the right hand river. At a waymark post (two paths are signed) take the right hand path to cut over the field to a hidden stile about 100 yards to the left of the far corner. A well-walked path goes through two fields to a churchyard.

This is Church Lawford's church, dedicated to St Peter. It was mainly rebuilt in the 19th century but parts of the much earlier fabric were incorporated including a Jacobean pulpit. Next to the church is the splendidly Tudor-timbered Manor Farm.

8. Go through the churchyard and through the gate. Cross to the opposite path and take the arrowed heading. In the diagonal corner climb a stile and take the right hand path to go over another stile. Turn left to retrace your steps along Smithy Lane, then right to the garden centre, or left to the inn.

Walk 8
HENLEY-IN-ARDEN

*T*he *Mount that overlooks Henley is not a mountain but a green hill in Beaudesert over which we walk at the start of this route. The castle site is a fine panoramic viewpoint throughout 360°. The route is then over further steep-sided ridges and across sheeplands. The little village of Preston Bagot with its 11th century hilltop church is visited. The path drops down to a lane passing a mossy seat on which you may decipher the carving 'Rest and be thankful' – so apt with the beautiful view across the vale. The return along fieldpaths to Henley and the welcoming café is across meadows where cattle and sheep graze.*

The premises of today's friendly, welcoming Henley Tea Rooms have been fronting the main highway in Henley-in-Arden since the 16th century, and in 1943 the manufacture of the famous Henley Ice Cream was started behind the teashop site. You are tempted to 'spoil yourself' on the sundaes and ice creams but walkers may resist and plump for the excellent range of sandwiches or teatime nibbles such as toasted crumpets and teacakes. For a lunchtime snack, there are also plenty of different fillings for baked potatoes. The café is open daily from 10 am to 6 pm for 50 weeks of the year (closed over Christmas and the New Year). Telephone: 01564 795172.

If the teashop is closed there are (as befits a market town) many pubs which are open all day, among them the Bluebell Inn which is at the Birmingham end of the High Street. Telephone: 01564 793049.

DISTANCE: 3½ miles.
MAP: OS Landranger 151 Stratford-upon-Avon, Warwick and Banbury.
STARTING POINT: High Street, Henley-in-Arden, by Beaudesert Lane (GR 152662).
HOW TO GET THERE: Henley-in-Arden is on the A3400 between Stratford-upon-Avon and Birmingham. Public car parks are signed, or you may be able to find streetside parking. The Henley Tea Rooms are on the High Street.

THE WALK

The café is in the main street of a town that has won several prizes in many 'Towns in Bloom' competitions. The street itself has been called 'a living museum of domestic architecture'. Nearby is the shaft of the market cross which dates from the 15th century. The Guildhall is much the same age.

1. From the High Street go down Beaudesert Lane beside the church. Go over the river to Beaudesert and pass the church.

The church of St Nicholas, Beaudesert is a Norman gem. There are exquisite carvings on the doorways; the place was built by Thurstan de Montfort in 1170 on an earlier Saxon site.

2. When the lane turns sharp right go through the gate ahead. The path goes over the Mount.

The castle here was also the work of Thurstan de Montfort and was built of wood and stone on the ancient site of a British fortified camp. He was granted the great privilege of a weekly market and annual fair by Empress Matilda (daughter of Henry I) in 1140.

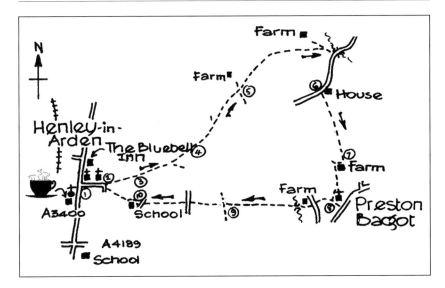

3. Follow the path along the ridge. Go down steps to a crossroads of paths. Walk directly over to climb the next ridge. At the summit several paths meet by stiles. Maintain the old direction by an old fieldgate. Within 250 yards go over a stile (rather hidden by a green metal gate) on the right. The stile is marked as being on the Heart of England Way.

The Heart of England Way is a long-distance footpath that runs from Cannock Chase in the north to Bourton-on-the-Water in Gloucestershire. It is about 100 miles in length.

4. Follow the arrowed direction diagonally over the open pasture to a far stile. On a wide track – perhaps an ancient highway – turn left. Within 100 yards bear right through bushes to a path over open arable land to a farm 'road'.

5. Cross directly over to a field and drop downhill along the left hand border. Go over a corner stile and walk through a little coppice then over the open pasture to a stile now seen. Walk down the middle of a large pasture to a stile just to the right of a row of cypress trees. Within a few steps climb another stile (house to the left). Keep the direction by a left hand hedge to a farm drive. Turn right to a road. Turn right.

41

Henley-in-Arden's attractive high street

6. Within 300 yards the road turns sharp right. A few steps further take a signed path through a gate left. Follow the arrowed direction to pass through a hunting gate. Keep ahead now climbing with woods away to the right. Go over a stile in the far left hand corner to a rough pasture and continue to another stile in the far right hand corner.

7. Immediately turn right over another stile. Follow the fenced way to go over a barrier. Turn left between a hedge (on the right) and fence (left). Pass through a metal gate by sheds. Keep ahead along a concrete way and pass through a field gate to a grassy paddock. Keep ahead to a corner kissing gate. Follow a left hand hedge and wooden fence to a gate to the churchyard.

All Saint's Church, Preston Bagot has a shingled bell turret but it is the Norman work that draws folk here. Sadly this is another country church that has to be kept locked but we can still admire the Norman windows and doorways – and the views! I am told that the architect placed a window so that the dipping evening sun makes the altar cross glow with light.

8. Retrace your steps out of the gate from the churchyard and follow the path over the grass to a kissing gate (by that mossy seat). Drop down the hill path to a lane. Cross directly over through a metal gate with a farmstead on the right. Walk alongside the hedge to go over a stile and plank bridge – watch out for mud! Keep ahead to the next stile. Bear right by a right hand hedge to a corner stile. Follow the direction of a waymark arrow over the open field to a step stile near the far left hand corner under an oak tree. Paths meet here – keep ahead alongside a right hand wire fence and hedge. Climb a corner stile and walk at the border of a plantation of saplings. There is another corner stile. Continue alongside a right hand wire fence and climb a stile. Over the next field walk across the open field, maintaining the old heading to a stile now seen.

9. On a wide track turn right for a few steps then climb a stile to a pasture left to regain the old heading. Climb a corner stile and keep the direction through gates to a lane. Turn right then at once left over a stile. In a pasture walk by a right hand border. Climb a corner stile then at once another. Drop down steps to a playing field. Go through a broken gate.

10. Walk along a fenced path to a road. Cross to the opposite path which goes around a school playing field. Do not go through a gate to the Mount but continue along the fenced path to reach Beaudesert Lane. Retrace your steps to the High Street and the Henley Tea Rooms.

Walk 9
COUGHTON COURT AND THE
RIVER ARROW

This pleasant walk can be combined with a visit to historic Coughton Court which, although included in the National Trust's list of properties, is lived in, opened and managed by the Throckmorton family. It has been their home since 1409. From the magnificent house the walk continues along the bank of the River Arrow. Few come this way so the wildfowl gather. We then come to the hamlet of Spernall, with its interesting redundant but retained church. A short section of lane walking leads to pathways over arable lands. Here the hilly terrain gives lovely views. Through a farm the walk edges woods where gamebirds scatter as we approach.

The Throckmorton Arms, just over the road from Coughton Court, is a splendidly restored inn that combines the old and the new. Do not be deterred by the busy road that runs at the front. All the activity is at the rear especially on sunny days – the terrace overlooks a lovely rural landscape. The food is simple but there is a wide choice. The ploughman's platter is especially good and is suitable for vegetarians. The chef offers a daily 'Special'; when I called it was squid as a starter and the more mundane but excellent sausage and mash. This freehouse always has an extensive selection of beers including Fuller's London Pride, Timothy Taylor's, Bass and a 'guest' – sometimes the intriguing Boneale. The pub is open every day from 12 noon to 11 pm. Telephone: 01789 766366.

There is also a tearoom at Coughton Court which is open when the house is open (April through to September although closed on some days of the week). It is best to check by telephoning 01789 762435. Note that access to the tea room is through the paying entrance to the property.

DISTANCE: 4½ miles.

MAP: OS Landranger 150 Worcester, The Malverns and surrounding area.

STARTING POINT: The car park at the Throckmorton Arms (GR 079609).

HOW TO GET THERE: Coughton is on the A435 between Redditch and Alcester. The Throckmorton Arms is on the west side of the main road. Alternatively, you could park by the ford (point 2) or at Coughton Court itself (entrance charge payable; free to NT members).

THE WALK

1. From the Throckmorton Arms cross the main road. Turn right. Within a few steps go through a metal kissing gate on the left. Cross the parkland to Coughton Court.

Coughton Court is renowned as one of England's great Tudor houses. The Throckmortons were instigators of Catholic emancipation and there is an interesting exhibition of the associations with the Gunpowder Plot. The magnificent gatehouse was the work of Sir George who died on a pilgrimage in 1518. There is much else to delay our walk including the walled garden (said to be England's finest), a bog garden and collections of portraits and memorabilia of the Throckmorton family over the centuries.

Turn right along the drive, passing two churches.

Both the churches were built by the Throckmorton family. St Peter's was built about 1450 on an earlier Saxon site. The family retained their Catholic faith

45

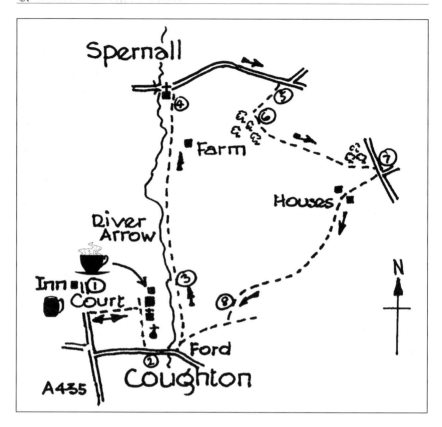

after the Reformation when the old church was taken over by the Anglicans. When the Roman Catholics could have their own places of worship again in the 19th century the family built the Catholic church in 1855.

2. On a lane turn left to pass the small parking area by the idyllic ford. Walkers can go over the footbridge. At once turn left along a vehicle way through a gate (signed as a cycle way). Immediately turn left across the grass. Keep at the side of the field with woods on the left. Go over a stile in a far corner and follow the arrowed way below a gentle right hand ridge.

3. Pass through a hunting gate by a National Trust sign. Maintain the heading and go over a substantial footbridge to an arable field. Follow the indicated way to nudge the riverbank to a fence gap in the far left

Coughton Court

hand corner. Over a plank bridge walk across an open field. Go over another plank bridge and through a gateway. Cross an open field to again meet the river. Follow the field edge to a broken fence to gain the next field. Note: the stile a few yards to the left is overgrown. Walk the length of a large sheep pasture. Aim just to the right of the church.

This is the former church dedicated to St Leonard. It is now owned by the Ancient Monument Society. The first rector was recorded in 1270 but the origins of the church may well be 12th century. The place is now closed for worship but is preserved by the Society because of the historic interest.

4. Go through a kissing gate to a farm drive which you follow to a lane. Turn right. Keep on the lane for about ½ mile.

5. Just past a right hand cottage and just before a junction take a signed path. Follow the arrowed direction over the open field, making for a point on the right hand end of an elongated wood.

6. Turn left to keep at the side of the trees, which are now on your right side. At the end of the wood cross a tractor way to go through a hedge gap. Continue over an open field to make for the far hedge gap now seen to the left of the woods. Go over a plank bridge. Bear left over the next open field. Leave the field under a double electricity pole. Climb the nearby stile to a pasture. Turn left to the cattle grid by the road.

7. Do not go over the cattle grid but along the drive (right) to farm buildings. Walk along the main track between the two houses. Keep ahead along the tractor way alongside right hand hedges. In a corner go through a wide hedge gap and over a wide concrete bridge. Beyond is a waymark arrow on a tree root. Continue with a hedge on the left side. The track passes to the right of the wooded Windmill Hill.

There are many Windmill Hills throughout the English countryside. Windmills were thought to have been invented by the Arabs in the 7th century and brought to this country by the returning Crusaders. As late as 1919 there were still 350 working mills but today there are little over a score.

8. Follow the clear tractor way to a stile by a metal gate. Cross a grassed area to a bold farm track. Turn right. The track leads to the gate by the ford. Retrace your steps to Coughton Court and the inn.

Walk 10
HATTON

This walk starts from the wonderful Hatton Country World where you will find numerous craft shops, animals and rural exhibitions – and two cafés! There is also a waymarked walk around the surrounding fields and countryside so if you do not have time for the circuit described here you could tackle the short stroll before tackling the tea! The route of my walk drops down beside the celebrated Hatton Flight – always interesting with wildfowl and gaily-painted holiday craft. There are then pathways beside woodlands and through farmland, with a section of country lane in between. The hills are generally quite gentle on the walk but there is a stiff climb up to Hampton on the Hill to give the reward of good views towards Warwick and its castle.

Hatton Country World is a joy, with so much to delight visitors of all ages: a wonderful Shopping Village with a wide assortment of craft shops, plenty of farm animals, birds and displays in the Farm Park, and adventure playgrounds where one hankers to be young again. But it also boasts two complementary eating places, both open daily from 10 am to 5 pm. The Greedy Pig Café Bar is licensed and offers full lunches besides teatime snacks. Its steak and ale pie and the Hatton Country World Sausages are well worth a visit on their own! The Café Lavender Blue offers lighter fare in a bright modern venue. There is a wide choice of excellent lunches (especially good salads) which can be enjoyed with a glass of wine. There are also tempting cakes to accompany that afternoon cup of tea. Added to all this is a farm shop where picnic snacks are available. One telephone number for all: 01926 843411.

DISTANCE: 5 miles.
MAP: OS Landranger 151 Stratford-upon-Avon, Warwick and Banbury.
STARTING POINT: The car park at Hatton Country World (GR 235663).
HOW TO GET THERE: 3 miles west of Warwick along the A4177 turn south on a lane signed to Hatton Country World.

THE WALK

1. After visiting the attractions of Hatton Country World walk back along the drive to the road. Turn right to the canal bridge and gain the towpath.

The construction in the early years of the 19th century of the Grand Union Canal had to contend with a gigantic engineering problem – the raising of the craft to the 350 ft high Midlands Plateau. The solution was the Hatton Flight – 21 locks over 2 miles of waterway. A gentle amble for walkers along the towpath but hard work for the boat crews.

2. On the towpath go under the road and continue with the water on your left side. At bridge number 64 cross over the canal and immediately regain the towpath, with the water now on your right.

The tall cupola peeping over distant trees is on buildings which were the County Asylum. This dates from 1852 and was built in brick in a Jacobean style. The lands are now used as a vast housing estate.

3. At the next bridge leave the canal. Cross the water. Follow the clear path then walk under a railway. Climb a stile to a well-worn path over

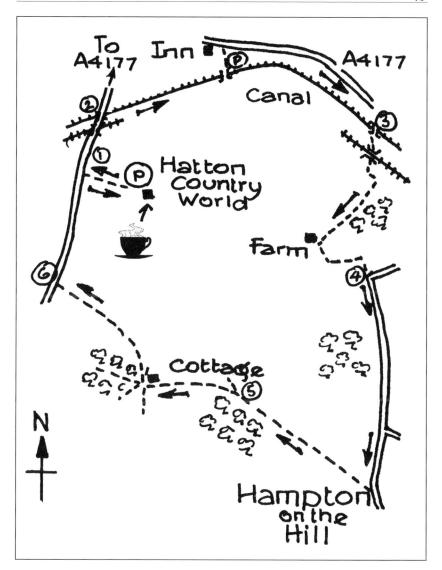

an arable field to a wood. Continue beside a right hand wire fence towards a farm. Turn left to walk along the drive.

On the distant horizon is Warwick. The church tower (174 ft high) is on St Mary's church and was built after a disastrous fire in 1694. We can also see the

The impressive flight of locks at Hatton

towers of Warwick Castle – Caesar's Tower (147 ft) and Guy's Tower (128 ft) to the right.

4. At a lane keep ahead and also at a junction. Climb the rise to Hampton on the Hill and continue through the village. As the lane bears left go right along the private road of Grove Park (a right-of-way footpath).

5. Go past cottages and a left hand wood. When the way divides take the left hand fork to cross the open field. At Wilderness Cottage the vehicle way turns sharp right and goes to a lane.

6. Turn right and walk along the lane to the entrance of Hatton Country World. Retrace your steps to the car park and those tempting cafés.

Walk 11
UFTON

The highlight of this walk is the Ufton Fields Nature Reserve. This area of over 30 hectares is owned by Warwickshire County Council and leased to the Warwickshire Wildlife Trust for everyone to enjoy. It is a Site of Special Scientific Interest (SSSI). Many unusual plants can be seen flourishing on the lime-rich soil including five kinds of orchid; in addition many species of butterfly and fifteen types of dragonfly find the conditions to their liking. We, for our part, are urged to leave nothing but footprints and take nothing but photographs.

 The White Hart, a 400 year old coaching house is on the main road through Ufton. The building has not always been an inn as it once housed stonemasons constructing St Michael's church nearby. On a fine day you may like to sit in the garden for the magnificent views across the Avon Vale. This is a pub that prides itself on the great variety of its fare. The menu is extensive and one of the all-time favourites – steak and Guinness pie – is particularly good. Red snapper, an unusual fish dish, is also popular. Real ales on offer include Adnam's Abbot and Tetley. The pub is open every day from 11.30 am to 3 pm and from 6 pm to 11 pm (10.30 pm on Sundays). Telephone: 01926 612428.

DISTANCE: 2½ miles.
MAP: OS Landranger 151 Stratford-upon-Avon, Warwick and Banbury.
STARTING POINT: The White Hart car park (GR 379622).
HOW TO GET THERE: Ufton is 4 miles south-east of Leamington Spa on the A425.

THE WALK

The village (recorded as Ulchtune in the 1086 Domesday Book) is on a high limestone ridge overlooking the vale in which the Fosse Way runs. The church is 14th century but was on a Saxon site; there is an old preaching cross in the churchyard. In past days the estate was owned by the Spencers of Althorp.

1. From the White Hart car park walk to the roundabout. Turn down the road called Ufton Fields.

Many buildings and walls built of a grey stone are passed. The stone is lias and on the walk you will see numerous waymark signs featuring symbols of fossils found in the rock. One celebrated, almost perfect fossil found in 1898 was of a ichthyosaurus and was over 19 ft in length; it was removed to the Natural History Museum.

2. Within ⅓ mile and as the lane twists sharp left take a path over a stile right. Follow the direction indicated across the open sheep pasture.

This path is part of the 100 mile Centenary Way that was created in 1989 to mark the 100th anniversary of the Warwickshire County Council. It runs from Kingsbury Water Park in the north of the county to south of Stratford-upon-Avon.

3. Go over a far stile. Maintain the heading (left hand hedge) to two corner stiles near a cottage. Turn left through a hedge gap. Continue at the side of an arable field (with the cottage now on your right) to a lane.

4. Turn left.

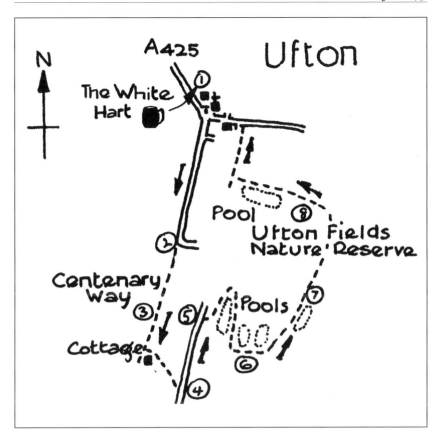

5. Within 500 yards turn right into the entrance of the Ufton Fields Nature Reserve. Leaflets are available here to add interest to your walk. Go through the car park. Walk along a bold path with Alder Pool on your right. Go around the other side of the pool through alder trees.

The landscape hereabouts was (up to the 1960s) scarred by quarries where limestone was extracted for the large cement works in the district. The vast amount of spoil was piled in ridges alongside the deep furrows. The work of nature took over when the work of man finished; the quarries filled with water and grasses and wild flowers thrived on the rough ridges.

6. Continue around Willow Pool and Little Grebe Pool. The path then twists around to the left to pass near Dragonfly Pool.

The duck pond at Ufton

There is a good hide here where the many types of dragonfly and wildfowl such as coots, moorhens and grebes can be observed. Do ensure that the covers to the viewing holes are replaced when you leave.

7. The clear path goes through Cowslip Clearing.

The works railway ran through this open area carrying the limestone away. Orchids (and of course cowslips!) thrive on the limey, grassed clearing and a little further an old quarry hopper lies rusting at the side of the path.

8. The path goes through the self-explanatory Butterfly Clearing. As you near houses a metal kissing gate is reached. Pass through the gate and follow a clear path at the border of a field and allotment. At the main road turn left to return to the inn.

Walk 12
SOUTHAM

*O*ne *guidebook says that Southam has a 'holy well that never freezes and a street that always pleases'. The town has some fascinating buildings too, including the gabled Olde Mint Inn. We stroll south along the High Street to start the walk, with a splendid view of the church that was built in the Perpendicular style in the 16th century – note the wonderful clerestory windows above the nave, which give a fine, bright interior to the building. The path then borders a fast-flowing tributary of the River Itchen, passing a holy well and an Elizabethan house. The river is crossed where the waters (which no doubt served a mill) tumble eagerly over a weir. The paths across rather lonely farmland go to the hamlet of Bascote. The return to Southam is along the valley of the Itchen.*

The Olde Mint Inn in Southam's High Street dates back to the 14th century. It takes its name from the Civil War when coins were minted here after the first battle of the conflict at Edge Hill in October

1642. King Charles I commanded local nobles to bring silver to be melted down to make coins to pay the surviving soldiers. While they waited they sharpened their swords and arrows on the stonework of the building. The pub is not artificial 'ye Olde English' – here is the real thing with massive timbers, stone-flagged floors and scrubbed tables. The food is certainly modern, and a splendid menu ranges from assorted snacks and salads to full meals and at least three vegetarian dishes. Youngsters love the Kid's Menu – plenty 'with chips', of course. There is a similarly wide choice of beers with Theakston ales featured. The pub is open all day, every day. Telephone: 01296 812339.

DISTANCE: 4½ miles.

MAP: OS Landranger 151 Stratford-upon-Avon, Warwick and Banbury.

STARTING POINT: The public car park (free) near the post office in the High Street. (GR 419620).

HOW TO GET THERE: Southam is 6½ miles south-east of Leamington Spa on the A425.

THE WALK

A stroll around the little town of Southam is a pleasant start to the walk. The valued charter was granted by Henry III in 1227 and developed into three separate markets for pigs, cattle and general goods. These resulted in a extraordinary number of inns. This was another resting place for Charles I; he stayed at the Manor House in 1642 before the Battle of Edgehill. The spire of St James's church has overlooked the town since the 15th century and there is an avenue of limes in the churchyard that commemorated the Battle of Waterloo. Shakespeare, too, knew the town – see the mention in Act V Scene I of Henry VI Part III.

1. From the car park walk along the High Street towards the church. Just past the library turn right down Park Lane. Beyond the churchyard go into a playing field left. Cross to the diagonal corner; pass through a kissing gate.

2. Keep the same heading along the vehicle way to pass to the right of an Air Training Corps centre. Go through a metal kissing gate. Walk over a pasture towards a footbridge across a brook. Do not cross but stay near the brook. Go through a far kissing gate and maintain the direction. Pass through railings to the Holy Well.

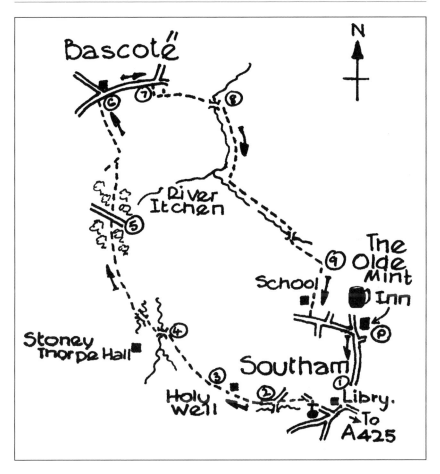

Holy wells are common throughout the country and many date from pre-Christian times when the never-ending supply of water was venerated. The water here was thought to have been a cure for eye ailments but (although I find no corroboration) to me the stone structure looks more like an ancient sheep dip!

3. Stay near the brook – the route is indicated by stiles and yellow arrows. Cross the bold bridge.

Nearby is a mansion that I found was boarded-up and crying out for rescue. The house is Stoney Thorpe Hall and dates from the 16th/17th century.

The attractive town of Southam

4. Over a stile follow a way by the left hand water. Cross a bridge and regain the old direction, now walking with water on each side. Climb a stile by a metal gate. Two paths are signed; keep ahead alongside a right hand hedge to a corner stile by a wood. Follow a clear path through the trees and over a bridge to a lane.

The lane here is the Welsh Road along which cattle were driven from Wales to London markets.

5. Cross to the opposite signed path. Climb the hill through the trees. In arable lands cross directly over the open field to pick up a right hand hedge. We reach a farm storage yard for old machinery. Follow the farm vehicle way around to the right – this leads to a lane.

6. Turn right to follow the lane through Bascote hamlet. Within 400 yards and, just before the lane twists sharp left, take a signed path through a gate by a barn on the right.

Bascote is memorable for some rare plants like butterfly orchis and green twayblade growing in local woods.

7. Climb the rise along the left hand border of the field. Go over a corner stile and turn left. At a waymark post take the path ahead over the open field to reach a bridge over the River Itchen.

There are at least two rivers in England called Itchen. The name probably comes from an Old English word related to the Iceni tribe.

8. Follow the border of the river upstream with waymarks showing the route. In a corner of a field turn left, so walking away from the river with a little stream on the right side. In a corner go over a plank bridge and stile. Follow the arrowed way, keeping to the left hand side of the field. Go through a corner gap (waymarked) and continue by a left hand hedge.

9. Near to some houses, go over a metal stile and take the footpath right. Pass by a school (on your right) to a road. Turn left (the Welsh Road again). At a T-junction turn right to Southam High Street.

Walk 13
ALCESTER

*T*he lovely buildings in the ancient town of Alcester (designated as a Conservation Area as long ago as 1967) may well delay you as you start this walk; Butter Street and Malt Mill Lane with its Tudor overhangs are especially attractive. A lane then takes you to the hamlet of Oversley Green; here there are pretty cottages, some capped by thatch. The route just nudges Exhall – 'Dodging Exhall' in a piece of doggerel about Shakespeare's villages. The return is over pastures where there are many inquisitive horses grazing. This is a delightful walk at any time of year, but I recommend it particularly in spring and autumn when the vast woods that you pass are at their glorious best.

The Three Cooks Bakery and Coffee Shop is in the middle of the main commercial area of Alcester and offers a welcome relief for the harassed shopper. The bakery emits that wonderful aroma of freshly made bread whilst one is enjoying the beverages and eats. The decor, based on sunshine yellow and light sky blue, gives a bright dining area. The colours are picked up again in the uniforms of the cheerful staff who obviously enjoy working together so well in this busy environment. There is a very comprehensive menu on a wall board behind the counter: filled baguettes and omelettes, for example, and a choice of six varieties of pasty. There are also plenty of wicked cream cakes. The Three Cooks is open daily from 9 am to 5 pm. Telephone: 01789 763826.

When the café is closed you will find several pubs nearby, among them the Royal Oak, an early 18th century listed inn, just a few steps away in the High Street. Telephone: 01789 762466.

DISTANCE: 4 miles.
MAP: OS Landranger 150 Worcester, The Malverns and surrounding area.
STARTING POINT: The Three Cooks Bakery and Coffee Shop (GR 090573).
HOW TO GET THERE: Alcester is just off the A435 south of Redditch. Park in one of the public car parks (charge) and make your way on foot to the café at the junction of Stratford Road and High Street in the centre of the town.

THE WALK

Alcester was Alauna to the Romans. Their Ryknild Street ran through the town and many relics from that era have been found – the building of a supermarket a score or so years ago uncovered a Roman building. The town hall on an island site dates from 1641 and the noble-looking church was here a couple of centuries earlier. Nothing remains, however, to tell us of the old abbey.

1. Out of the café turn left along the High Street. Opposite the church go along the exquisite Malt Mill Lane. Around a bend take a tarmac path over the grass left. On the main road cross and turn left. Immediately turn right along a road signed to Oversley Green. Cross a bridge.

There are six arches of the bridge which was built in 1600. Nearby the rivers Arrow and Alne merge to flow to the Avon and the Bristol Channel.

2. Bear right at the little green then left by a picturesque thatched cottage to walk along Primrose Lane. At the end walk along a metal-railed footpath to cross a bridge over a main road. By a stile (do not climb) turn left along a tarmac path. Within 100 yards go through a gate to a vehicle way.

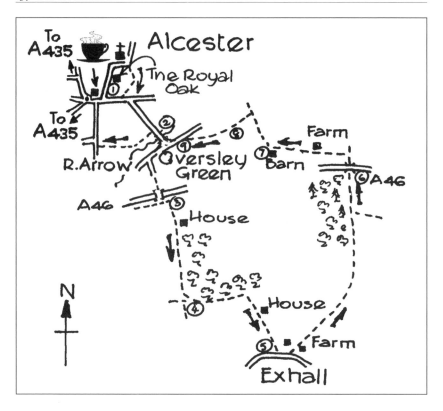

3. Cross to the path opposite which leads to another vehicle way. Turn right to climb the hill. By an elegant gateway pass through white gates to keep ahead along a bridleway that soon borders the left hand Oversley Woods.

On a wooded hill to the right is the white Oversley Castle. It was the Prince Regent visiting the Marquis of Hertford's Ragley Hall who remarked that the view from his front door would be improved by a castle. The 2nd Marquis took up the suggestion and promptly built the folly.

4. At a corner of the woods is a waymark post showing several paths. Turn left to follow a track just in the woods with arable lands to the right. Within 400 yards there is another waymark post. Turn right alongside a right hand hedge. Go through a gate and continue past a house. Follow the drive to a lane at Exhall.

5. Turn left then at once left again. The bridleway is signed along a farm way. Keeping on the main way go past barns. Maintain the heading along a tractor way, passing through gates. When the tractor way ends at two gates side by side go through the left hand one. In a pasture walk by a right hand hedge. Go through a far metal hunting gate then follow alongside left hand woods to reach a main road.

6. Cross a stile and walk by a car park area to go under the main road. At once turn left over a stile by a gate. Walk along a tractor way and keep ahead near the farm. Climb a stile by a metal gate and continue along a fenced way.

7. Pass a pool and a left hand barn. Go through a corner metal gate. Bear right to walk alongside a right hand wire fence. At a corner there is a stile. Do not climb this but turn left to walk at the side of a wire fence and golf practice area.

8. Go through a corner gate. Stay by the wire fence. Climb a corner stile then take the arrowed direction over the pasture. Climb a stile tucked in a corner. Walk at the bottom of gardens to a road at Oversley Green.

9. Turn left to pass the green where we were before. Cross the bridge, then 150 yards further on take a signed path through a kissing gate on the left. Follow the border of a sports field. Pass through another kissing gate and follow the arrowed way. The path nears the river and stays by the left hand boundaries of fields to a stile to a road. Turn right to return to Alcester.

Walk 14
WILMCOTE

*T*he village of Wilmcote would probably have been unknown had it not been for Mary Arden's House. No main road passes through and the canal brings only silent holiday craft winding their leisurely way to Stratford. However, Wilmcote is now firmly on the Shakespeare tourist trail and many visitors come from far and near. The route of the walk soon leaves the tourists behind as we go northwards along the canal towpath. The narrow waterway twists a delightful passage through the pastoral countryside with constantly changing views. Beyond the hamlet of Newnham the track climbs the upland called Rough Hills which were once extensively quarried for building stone. A short road walk precedes another steep climb up the ridge on which Wilmcote stands, with a final flat pathway back to the start.

The tearoom attached to Mary Arden's House and Museum is situated – in contrast to the 16th century farmhouse – in modern and airy premises. As it is part of the Drucker's chain of restaurants so well known in the Midlands there is, not surprisingly, an elegant style about the place, with cane chairs and little round tables. Original paintings (which are for sale) by local artists are on the walls. Drucker's celebrated cream gateaux are very tempting but there is such a choice of cakes, strudels and pastries that 'make your mind up time' can be difficult. Light snacks are also offered, such as filled croissants and rolls and savouries. The tearoom is open daily (as is Mary Arden's House) from 9.30 am to 5 pm (summer months) and 10 am to 4 pm (winter months, mid October to mid March). Telephone: 01789 267730.

Alternatively you could visit the Mason's Arms in the centre of the village, a few steps along the Aston Cantlow road – a typical English village pub, where everything is home made. Telephone: 01789 297416.

DISTANCE: 4 miles.
MAP: OS Landranger 151 Stratford-upon-Avon, Warwick and Banbury.
STARTING POINT: The car park of the café at Mary Arden's House (GR 165583).
HOW TO GET THERE: Wilmcote is 4 miles north-west of Stratford-upon-Avon and signed off the A3400. Mary Arden's House is at the start of the village on the right.

THE WALK

In 2001 an amazing piece of research determined that the real Mary Arden's House was not the residence of Shakespeare's mother that had been shown to eager tourists for many years but the place next door – a shame really as the true house is less photogenic! The place also houses a museum of country artefacts.

1. Out of the car park turn left on the road. At the canal bridge gain the towpath and continue with the water on your left.

This is the Stratford-upon-Avon Canal which was built 200 years ago to carry coal southwards and limestone northwards. The waterway is 15 miles long and today a favourite circuit for leisure craft is Stratford Canal – River Avon – River Severn – Worcestershire Canal and back to the Stratford Canal.

2. Go past one bridge.

Note the split down the middle of the bridge which enabled horses to pass the bridge without the necessity of unhitching from the barges being towed.

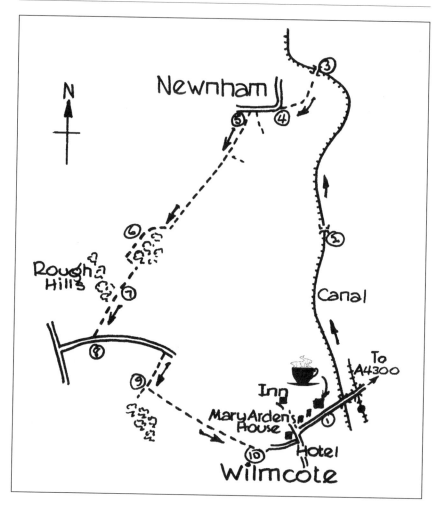

3. At the next bridge leave the canal. Cross the water past a rusty gate to a field. Follow the right hand border. Within 300 yards go over a plank bridge right then over the nearby step stile to a pasture. Follow the arrrowed heading to climb a stile in the opposite fence. Maintain the direction to pass through a gateway (stile overgrown) to a lane.

4. Turn left to the village of Newnham.

5. Just before the little green take a path signed down a vehicle way on the left. It is also signed 'Meadow Barn'. Ignoring other paths keep ahead along the vehicle drive to pass houses and a green barn. Beyond the barn walk along the tractor way beside left hand hedges. At the top of a rise you are directed right (still by the left hand hedge) to pass through a corner hunting gate.

6. The bridleway now borders abandoned left hand quarries.

The quarries supplied extensive quantities of a hard building stone which can be seen in the surrounding villages like Aston Cantlow. The area is now an SSSI – a Site of Special Scientific Interest – and administered by the Nature Conservancy Council.

7. Stay at the border of the huge upland pasture to pass through a rather hidden new hunting gate in a corner by a wood. Follow the clear path which drops down to a road.

8. Turn left and climb the hill. At the top take an unmade-up lane (Marsh Road) on the right.

9. Within 400 yards take a signed path through a hunting gate on the left. Follow the direct path through another gate and at the borders of fields.

10. At the far end of a sports field keep ahead along a fenced way to an estate road. Turn right and follow the road to a T-junction. Turn left then right to the tearoom at Mary Arden's House.

Walk 15
CHARLECOTE

*T*his *walk may be started by a stroll through the lovely parkland of Charlecote (National Trust). You can see the numerous deer and so muse on whether Shakespeare was really mocking Sir Thomas Lucy when he invented Mr Justice Shallow – the Bard was punished for stealing one of Sir Thomas's deer. The outward route of the walk is along the bank of the meandering River Dene to Wellesbourne. Ducks love this stretch of the river, finding plenty of cover in the hanging willows and reed beds. The return is similarly over a level landscape (there are no hills on this walk) along a lane and footpath.*

The tearoom (or coffee shop if you prefer!) is inside the excellent Charlecote Garden Centre. The range of food is limited – just light cold snacks – but this is an exceptionally pleasant setting, in the midst of lovely flowers and foliage. The tearoom is open daily from 10 am to 5 pm. Telephone: 01789 841842.

For something rather more substantial, a few steps away from the garden centre is the Charlecote Pheasant inn which serves lunches and dinners. It is best to telephone in advance: 01789 279954.

DISTANCE: 2½ miles. (plus a stroll in the park if you wish).
MAP: OS Landranger 151 Stratford-upon-Avon, Warwick and Banbury.
STARTING POINT: The car park in the Charlecote Garden Centre (GR 263563).
HOW TO GET THERE: Turn off the A429 north of Wellesbourne, signed to Charlecote. There are several parking options: the NT car park by the entrance to the park, the Charlecote Pheasant car park (patrons), the layby near the inn or the Charlecote Garden Centre car park.

THE WALK
Charlecote Park has been the seat of the Lucy family for seven centuries. The Tudor house was built by Sir Thomas in the form of a letter 'E' to flatter his monarch Elizabeth I. She spent time here on her way to Kenilworth. Much of the lovely interior dates from early Victorian times and the deer park was to the design of 'Capability' Brown. This is a National Trust property so there is an entrance fee. For details of opening times, telephone: 01789 470277.

1. Out of the garden centre car park turn left along the road. Cross the River Dene over a fine bridge. Within 200 yards take a signed path through a gateway left.

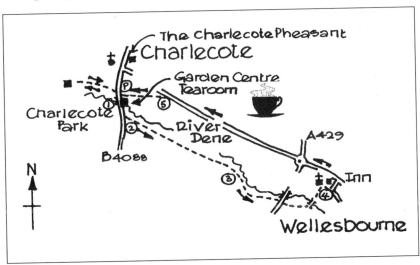

One of the delightful statues in Charlecote Park Gardens

2. Walk along a fenced way. At a metal gate (do not go through) turn left past an obsolete metal kissing gate then follow the riverside path.

Away to the right are the hangers and buildings of Wellesbourne airfield. This was built at the start of the Second World War in 1940 and was used to train aircrew on Wellingtons and Ansons. The RAF have gone but the place is busy with light private planes.

3. Pass through a metal kissing gate and stay by the river. Go under a road bridge and walk along a well-used path. When this splits keep on the main path to a tarmac path. Turn left to cross the river over a metal bridge. Follow the path through a gate to a churchyard. Keep the church on your left.

St Peter's church at Wellesbourne was mainly rebuilt in the 19th century although it is thought to have been on a Norman site. The tower has been looking over the village for 500 years. There is a brass to Sir Thomas le Strange depicting him as a knight in armour.

4. Pass out of the churchyard to a cul de sac lane. Turn right then at once left down Hopper's Lane. At the end turn left (Charlecote Road). At the roundabout take care crossing to the lane opposite. Keep ahead.

The fields to the right are marked into sections and there are distant greenhouses. These are the lands of a large horticulture research station. Here scientists work on problems connected with the raising of vegetables; they also preserve old varieties in a special genes bank.

5. Within ¾ mile take a signed path through a metal kissing gate on the left. Walk alongside a tall left hand hedge and through a rather unusual lift stile to a road. The Charlecote Garden Centre car park is to the left.

Walk 16
WELLESBOURNE

*T*his walk explores the valley of a tiny river; the Dene meanders its languid way as if in no hurry to be swallowed up by Shakespeare's Avon. The waters were well used by the creators of the extensive gardens of Walton Hall and the river was widened to form a lake, which you will cross. The Hall, built in the Gothic Revival style, was the inspiration in 1862 of Sir George Gilbert Scott. Our return is along the Dene valley passing an idyllic spot by a deep ford.

 The teashop is part of the wonderfully restored Wellesbourne Watermill. It is housed in a barn – the timber-framed building dates from the 18th century. The menu is quite modest but the food is all home-made and has an individual quality. The ploughman's lunch would not disappoint a farm worker of old and the assorted filled rolls are really full! For those who don't care, the wicked cream tea is a must. The teashop is open when the mill is open: 10 am to 4.30 pm from April to September on Thursday to Sunday inclusive. Telephone: 01789 470237. When the mill is closed refreshments can be obtained from the thatched Stag's Head pub at Wellesbourne which is almost on the route. There is always a wide range of beer here, including Whitbread, Boddingtons and Marston's ales. The food consists of good fare such as soups, 'with chips' dishes and well-filled baguettes and sandwiches. The Stag's Head is open from 11.30 am to 2.30 pm and 6 pm to 11 pm weekdays and 12 noon to 3 pm and 7 pm to 10.30 pm on Sundays. Telephone: 01789 840266.

DISTANCE: 4½ miles.

MAP: OS Landranger 151 Stratford-upon-Avon, Warwick and Banbury.

STARTING POINT: The car park at Wellesbourne Watermill (GR 285545).

HOW TO GET THERE: Wellesbourne is signed off the A429 south of Warwick. From the village go south-east along the B4086 to reach the mill and tearoom on the right after almost a mile.

ALTERNATIVE STARTING POINT: (when the mill is closed): Quiet road by the Stag's Head in Wellesbourne (GR 278552), just south of the B4086. You would then join the walk at point 3.

THE WALK

Before setting out do visit the fascinating mill. This is one of the few in the country where you can still see the machinery in action. You can watch ground wholemeal flour being produced – and then buy it if you wish. This is a 'hands on' experience for all the family. There is also a working blacksmith on the site. The swans glide on the millpond and a Welsh coracle glides through the rushes. On a warm summer's day it is almost too soporific for a walk!

1. From the tearoom go along the track towards the mill. Within a few steps an arrowed path crosses our track. Turn right to climb a stile behind stables. In a pasture turn right to walk alongside a right hand fence. Go through a metal gate to bear left over the field to cross the railed bridge now seen.

2. Go over the little River Dene. Follow the border of a sometimes arable field to a step stile to a pasture. Walk alongside a left hand fence then maintain the direction by an old field boundary. Continue ahead to pass through a kissing gate. There is now a fenced path. Pass

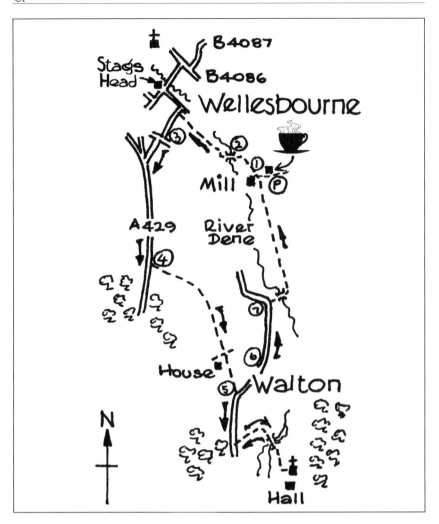

through a little gate then walk along a vehicle way to Lowes Lane. Turn left. (The Stag's Head and alternative starting place are to the right then immediately left.)

We are now on the borders of the growing village of Wellesbourne. The old heart has the 15th century church and the Malt House. The flat lands to the west were used to build a vast airfield during the Second World War. It was a training base for mainly Commonwealth airmen. After the war a small civilian airfield was established. There is also a Vulcan bomber which at present is being restored and does noisy test ground runs.

3. At a T-junction go right then left within 20 yards. As this road bears right to the main road keep ahead along the pathway. At the main road turn left. (There is a pavement part of the way and then a grass verge but take care as the road is quite busy.)

4. After ⅓ mile and just as the road begins to rise take a signed bridleway through a gate on the left. Now in arable lands walk alongside a left-hand hedge. Through a gate by a bungalow join a house drive.

5. At a lane turn right then left through the gateway of Walton Hall.

Since the heady days of the 19th century when the Mordaunt family lived here Walton Hall has had a chequered history. Lucky army units tried the grand style in the Second World War, then the Czech forces. Our troops reoccupied it, then a girls' school followed by a hotel (owned by Danny la Rue). The place is now divided into timeshare apartments but it retains a sweet little 18th century church.

Follow the drive over the distinctive way across the Dene called Gog Bridge to the little church.

The church of St James was rebuilt in 1750 by Sir Charles Mordaunt with a Tuscan porch. Nearby is the great hall which has a splendid long colonnade to the garden and bath house thought to be the work of Sanderson Miller.

6. Retrace your steps along the drive to the lane and turn right to go through the little village of Walton.

Walton is an estate village with a distinctive common building style. There are fifteen cottages and a forge and a school (with a missing bell and no longer calling late pupils) and the old laundry.

7. Just past the Walton village sign turn right. Go over the footbridge by the ford and climb a stile to the pasture on the left. Walk directly away from the stile alongside a right hand hedge. A series of stiles and waymark arrows lead back to Wellesbourne Mill and the barn tearoom.

Walk 17
BIDFORD-ON-AVON

*T*his was a place that Shakespeare knew: there is a rhyme about the Bard which calls the village 'Drunken Bidford' and certainly he came this way with his mates on drinking bouts at the Falcon Inn (the building is still there but is now a private house). He must have stood on the eight-arch bridge that we cross to reach the Bull's Head. The tower of the parish church is old too and has been gazing across the water meadows for over 700 years. The route follows the Avon for a mile or two to Cleeve Prior. Once a bustling wharf was here when the river was a commercial artery. We then continue past the Norman church and a historic Manor House. The pathways along the ridgetop are over mixed farmlands then drop down the escarpment to the hamlet of Marlcliff. Easy tracks (which can be muddy after rain, so go well shod) lead back to the car park by the ancient bridge.

The Bull's Head is in Bidford's main square. This is a pub that tongue in cheek undersells itself: 'We sell bad food, warm beer with bad service!' – don't believe a word of it. This is a popular place with locals who could easily go elsewhere! Try the Sunday lunch – just like mother's. If you qualify there is an excellent senior citizens' meal on weekdays, and I can also recommend the lunch that would have satisfied the hungriest of ploughmen in days past. There are cosy bars but the patio is a delight on warm days. The main beer is Tetley's but others are available. This pub is open all day, every day. Telephone: 01789 772242.

DISTANCE: 5 miles.
MAP: OS Landranger 150 Worcester, The Malverns and surrounding area.
STARTING POINT: The public car park (free) by Bidford Bridge (GR 100517).
HOW TO GET THERE: Bidford is 6½ miles west of Stratford along the B439. Take the B4085 south over the river to reach the car park on the right.

THE WALK

1. From the car park walk alongside the River Avon through the recreational meadow. Go through corner fence gaps and over stiles, keeping near the water on the right to reach a vehicle way.

A notice board here tells us that we have been walking along the Marlcliff Avon Footpath which runs by the Avon for 9 miles from Stratford. The path was opened by Christopher Hall, the then Chairman of the Ramblers' Association, on 27th June 1987.

2. Turn right through a car park and along the vehicle way, passing a lock on the river.

The land for the lock and weir was given to the Upper Navigation Trust by the Birmingham Anglers' Association – which some say is the largest angling club in the world. The navigation on the Avon was only restored a decade or so ago. A generous donation from the Inland Waters Association enabled the Royal Engineers, men from Gloucester Gaol and other volunteers to build the lock in July/August 1969.

3. Past the lock climb a stile and continue the walk beside the river which curves around a gentle bend to another stile and yellow waymark arrow. Within a step or so is another stile (rather obsolete) and old steps to another riverside path. Continue to a landscaped area with seats.

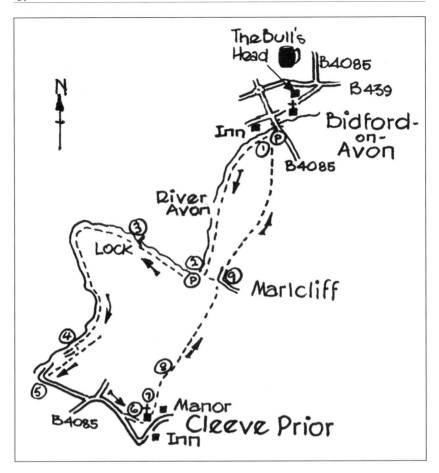

This is Cleeve Prior Parish Wharf, once an important commercial centre with an adjacent mill. It is also said that many of Simon de Montfort's soldiers perished in the river here after fleeing from the Battle of Evesham in 1265.

4. On the lane take the signed path left up steep steps to climb the escarpment. At the top turn right – a vehicle way to a lane.

Nearby is the Cleeve Prior Nature Reserve created by the County Council in association with the Worcestershire Wildlife Trust. The habitat has nurtured a wide variety of plant life, including milk vetch, purple loosestrife and arrowhead.

A glimpse of Bidford through one of the bridge arches

5. Turn left on the lane then left at the B4085 to walk through Cleeve Prior village. At the little green bear left along the vehicle way towards the church.

A tree on the green was planted to mark the 40th anniversary of the accession of Elizabeth II. There used to be a 300 year old elm on the green but that perished with the onset of Dutch Elm Disease.

6. Go through the gate into the churchyard and take a path to the left of the tower.

Cleeve Prior was named after the priors of Worcester Cathedral. St Andrew's church is built of the attractive local grey stone. There are Norman arches and the tower is 15th century. Are the scratches on the south-west buttress where archers sharpened their arrows? Other marks are a sundial to tell the time of the services.

7. Go through a hedge gap between tall poplar trees. Walk over the grass to a stile to leave the churchyard and continue over a meadow.

The Manor House on the right is said to have concealed Thomas Bushell in a hiding place in Stuart times; he supplied Charles I with money when the Royal Mint was in the hands of the Parliamentarians. When he died he was buried in Westminster Abbey 'for services to the Nation'.

8. Go over a plank bridge and a stile. Keep ahead alongside a left hand hedge. Climb a corner stile and maintain the heading. Go over another corner stile and still walk ahead (right hand hedge now). In a far corner turn left. Within 200 yards turn right alongside an old orchard. At the end keep ahead over the open field to a stile now seen. In a pasture bear left to a corner stile and continue to a stile above the escarpment. Drop down steps to a gate to a lane at Marlcliff.

9. Maintain the heading. At the end of the lane continue along a walled footpath to a stile to a field. Go alongside a left hand hedge and over a far corner stile. Maintain the direction. Within 300 yards go over a plank bridge left. At once turn right to walk at the border of a field. Cross the next field along a well-walked path to a kissing gate to a sports field. Follow the right hand border to the car park.

Walk 18
EDGE HILL AND UPTON HOUSE

The walk starts at the interesting Castle Inn on the ridge of Edge Hill. There is an early reclaimed path over ground that was once extensive quarries; it is hereabouts that the famous Hornton stone is found. We then go over land that dips and rises to give added beauty, then by a farmstead before continuing to Upton House, a fascinating National Trust property, open in the summer months. The return is on a bold path through woods.

 The Castle Inn has two great assets – its fantastic setting which gives lovely views over the Warwickshire Plain, and the history of the location. The site of the great Civil War battle of 23rd October 1642 is in the valley below the beech-clad slopes; unfortunately, it cannot be visited as it is on highly secret Ministry of Defence land. However, it was by the pub that Charles I raised the royal banner before the first fight of the war.

The pub is in a tower that was built as a sham castle by Sanderson Miller; it is a copy of Guy's Tower of Warwick Castle. There is much military memorabilia in the bars to stimulate any flagging conversation. This is a Hook Norton Brewery house with their usual range of beers but guest ales are also available. The pub is not on any main road so (without much passing trade) the place depends on reputation and recommendation. For hungry walkers the mixed grill is a good choice – especially if you can include the home-cured gammon! Vegetarians are well catered for too. The Castle Inn is open daily although the hours can be variable – best to check if outside the normal pub times. Telephone: 01295 670255.

DISTANCE: 4 miles.

MAP: OS Landranger 151 Stratford-upon-Avon, Warwick and Banbury.

STARTING POINT: The Castle Inn car park, Edge Hill (GR 373475).

HOW TO GET THERE: 12 miles south-east of Stratford-upon-Avon on the A422 take a lane northwards, signed to Edge Hill. You will reach the Castle Inn after about a mile.

THE WALK

1. Out of the car park opposite the pub turn right. Within a few steps take a signed post by a post box. The fenced path leads to a road. Turn right for 30 yards then cross the road. Walk along a farm way which is signed as a footpath.

The fenced plantation of young trees on the right was once a quarry for Hornton stone. Now the area has been reclaimed. Upton House was built of this local stone.

2. Climb a stile in the corner at the end of the track then immediately climb another. In a field turn right to pass a metal gate. Walk alongside a right hand hedge. Go over a corner stile. Maintain the heading (still by a right hand hedge) to pass through a metal gate. We are now heading towards a farmhouse.

3. When about 40 yards from a wall by the house turn 90 degrees left alongside a wire fence. Climb a corner stile by barns. Walk alongside a wall. Go through trees then at the edge of an arable field to a lane.

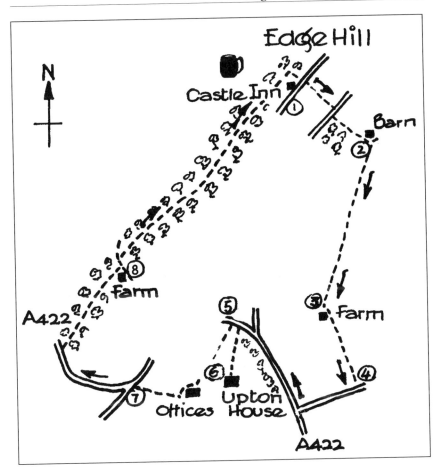

4. Turn right to the A422. Cross the road and turn right. Within 400 yards we reach the entrance to Upton House.

Upton House was given to the National Trust in 1948 by the 2nd Viscount Bearsted. He was chairman of Shell Oil and there is an interesting collection of posters and paintings commissioned by that company. In addition many paintings by English and Continental Old Masters and old furniture, porcelain and tapestries are on display. You can also have a stroll around the lovely gardens. The terraced lands make the most of the sloping grounds and there are water gardens that were constructed in the 1930s.

Upton House is now in the care of the National Trust

The property is open from April to the end of October, daily except Thursdays and Fridays. An entrance charge is payable (free to NT members). The teashop there serves scrumptious home-made cakes. Telephone: 01295 670266.

5. A few steps further and by a vehicle drive climb a stile to a sheep pasture.

6. Walk the length of the bumpy field (where stone has been extracted). Pass through a wooden gate then a metal gate. Follow the arrow aiming to the right of buildings. Go through a metal gate and over rough railings. Walk along the top of a bank (buildings on the left) to a car park. Go to the diagonal corner. Climb a fence stile by a gate. Follow a tractor way to pass through a gate. Keep along the track to pass through a white-topped gate to the A422.

7. Cross the road and turn left. Walk past a layby and a phone box. Turn right along a signed path into woodlands. Follow the path which runs along the right hand border of the woods. Soon pass a reassuring

Edge Hill

waymark arrow on a post. Go alongside a right hand wall by a farmstead.

8. At a vehicle way go left for 50 yards. Turn right along a signed path into woods. Keep ahead when another path joins. Just beyond our path divides. Take the right hand fork to climb steps then soon drop down steps and maintain the heading. At a bold meeting of signed paths bear right to go up the slope alongside a guide rail. At the top keep ahead at a crossing path to climb steps to a road and the pub.

Although this is a pub closely associated with the Civil War there are reminders inside of a more recent conflict. We are told of the first experimental jet aircraft (called the Pioneer) which had many test flights in 1942 from the nearby remote Shenington Aerodrome.

Walk 19
SHIPSTON-ON-STOUR AND BARCHESTON

From Sheep Street in the interesting old town of Shipston (from the Anglo-Saxon meaning 'the settlement-at-the sheepwash') we go over the river (one of the six Stours in England) and follow the valley through meadows to the little village of Barcheston, which has a Pisa-like leaning tower on its Norman church. Narrow lanes and an attractive fieldpath lead us back to the town and its many delights.

Hatties teashop looks down Sheep Street towards the castellated Georgian Manor House from its corner site by the old Market Place. This part of the road was once Cobblers Row. It is pleasant to look at the world going by as you sit in the sought-after window seats. The light lunches here include a fine selection of cold meats and salads – an unhurried meal in nice surroundings. The teas with home-made cakes are a wonderful reward for completing the walk. Hatties is open daily Monday to Saturday from 10 am to 5 pm but closed on Sundays. Telephone: 01608 662217.

There are about half a dozen pubs in the centre of Shipston if you do this walk when the teashop is not open, among them the Horseshoe Inn by the church. Its hours are from 11 am to 3 pm and 6 pm to 11 pm on Monday to Friday, 12 noon to 3 pm and 7 pm to 10.30 pm on Sunday and all day on Saturday. Telephone: 01608 661225.

DISTANCE: 2½ miles.

MAP: OS Landranger 151 Stratford-upon-Avon, Warwick and Banbury.

STARTING POINT: Telegraph Street (fee paying) car park well signposted from the A3400. (GR 259407).

HOW TO GET THERE: Shipston-on-Stour is 10 miles south of Stratford-upon-Avon along the A3400.

THE WALK

Shipston founded its fortunes on wool with a stock market continuing well into the 20th century. After the wealth from sheep the feudal society ended. The place became an important coaching town when the London to Birmingham Turnpike was built in 1730. This brought trade to the handsome inns like the George Hotel and the White Bear. There are memories of the age of wool in names such as Sheep Street. Shipston's church is quite modern (19th century) but has an ancient tower which has guarded the busy highway for almost six hundred years. There is a peal of six fine bells which has to compete with the traffic noise.

1. From the car park go through the passageway to Sheep Street then past the teashop and along the High Street to West Street. Turn left then right along Mill Street, following the direction of traffic (the main road). Within a few steps bear left. This is still Mill Street and is the B4035 signed to Brailes.

The old mill is now a nicely converted hotel and restaurant. It was a corn mill with plenty of water from the River Stour.

2. Go over the bridge across the river.

The bridge (half stone and half brick) has a datestone on its downstream side reading 'bilt 1698'. The old sheepwash which was so important was a ford just

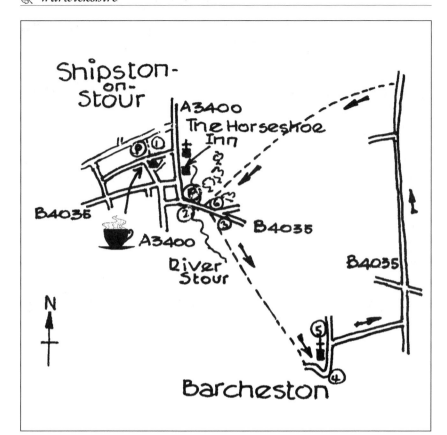

to the south of the bridge. In 1826 the width of the bridge was doubled to accommodate the increased coaching traffic.

3. About 200 yards past the bridge, by a road junction, cross the road to climb a stile to a meadow. Follow the path by the right hand border of the field to climb a corner stile. Walk over the open field to cross a double stile. Continue below electricity lines to the next stile. Over this follow the indicated direction to climb a stile by a gate. Join a vehicle way which becomes a lane and turn left.

We are now in Barcheston. There are only a handful of cottages and farmsteads today but history was made here. It was in 1561 that William Sheldon set up his famous tapestry looms at Manor House Farm.

St Martin's church, Barcheston

4. The lane bears left and across the green is the lychgate to St Martin's church.

The 14th century church tower is leaning about 1 foot in 50 but is said to have been at the same angle now for two centuries. There are many interesting monuments and the west window telling the story of St Martin is very fine.

5. At a junction take the lane right then turn left at a T-junction. Cross over the B4035 to the opposite lane. The lane climbs then passes a junction with Fell Mill Lane. About 200 yards further go along a wide farm track left. This soon bears left to become a footpath over arable land. Follow the well-walked path then go along the path through woods.

6. Follow the path to the B4035. Turn right. Retrace your steps to the tearoom or pub and the car park in Telegraph Street.

Walk 20
SHIPSTON-ON-STOUR, BARCHESTON AND TIDMINGTON

This walk starts through meadows along the banks of the River Stour where wildfowl such as swans and a variety of ducks gather. Through the tiny village of Barcheston, with its leaning tower, we continue over fields to reach a bold footbridge and cross the river. The walk again joins the Stour to emerge on a main road at Tidmington. The church (one of the smallest in the diocese) has a Norman tower and beside it is the rather splendid Tidmington House which has been on this site since the 17th century. The route from Tidmington is along narrow rural lanes with a fine long bridleway over the hills back to Shipston.

Country Kates' Kitchen at 14 Sheep Street is just right for walkers – it is at the back of a bakery and confectioner's and has a real rural feel about it. The decor is simple with about a dozen tables (all different!) with a vase of fresh flowers: like some Continental eating places you can peer into the kitchen to see what is cooking! The bill of fare is to the taste of walkers too – such things as an all-day breakfast, filled jacket potatoes and toasted sandwiches. The soup is home-made and tasty and very modestly priced. Country Kates' Kitchen is open from 7 am to 5.30 pm Monday to Saturday. Telephone: 01608 661563.

There is a good choice of pubs in the centre of Shipston, although many more were in business when there was a great sheep market in the town; some now converted into dwellings have retained their old pub names. As well as the Horseshoe Inn (see Walk 19) you will find excellent food at the Coach and Horses, just off the Square in New Road, where ramblers are given a warm welcome. The opening hours are from 12 noon to 3 pm and 6 pm to 11 pm on Monday to Thursday, and all day on Friday, Saturday and Sunday. Telephone: 01608 661335.

DISTANCE: 5 miles.

MAP: OS Landranger 151 Stratford-upon-Avon, Warwick and Banbury.

STARTING POINT: The free car park near the bridge over the Stour (GR 259405).

HOW TO GET THERE: Shipston-on-Stour is 10 miles south of Stratford-upon-Avon along the A3400. For the car park near the bridge make your way to the B4035 going east towards Upper Brailes.

THE WALK

Shipston-on-Stour is an old market town founded on sheep (with at one time one of the greatest sheep markets in the kingdom) and well worth perambulation before or after tackling the walk. The church of St Edmund has a 15th century tower and you will see fine Georgian buildings around the High Street (which is really the market place). There are narrow streets with rather old-fashioned but pleasant shops.

1. From the car park cross the river over the bridge. By a road junction go over the road to climb a stile to a meadow. Follow the path by the right-hand border of the field to climb a corner stile. Walk over the open field to go over a double stile. Continue below electricity lines to the next stile. Over this follow the indicated direction to climb a stile by a gate. Join a vehicle way which becomes a lane.

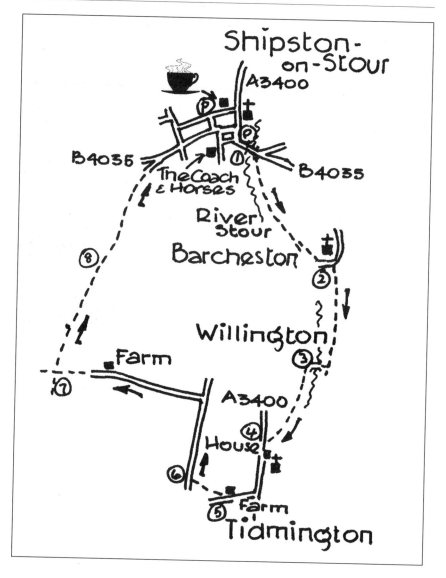

We are now in Barcheston which is famous for two things – its leaning church tower and the home of English tapestry. In the Manor House in the late 16th century Richard Hickes was employed by William Sheldon to put into practice the skills learnt on his trip to the Low Countries.

Shipston-on-Stour has many fine Georgian buildings

2. Within a few steps and as the lane twists sharp left take a signed path through a gateway on the right. Follow a straight path over the open field, never far from the river on the right, to a far stile. Several paths are signed here. Take the path ahead over the ridge and furrow field. Over a stile keep ahead to pass through a gate by a bridge.

Ridges and furrows indicate ancient strip farming which can be traced back as far as the Saxon invaders. The strips would have been a furlong (220 yards) in length and a chain (22 yards) wide to make an acre of land.

3. Turn right over the river and immediately go left. Keep near the river until a bend then veer right to a stile now seen in a fence. Gradually leave the left hand river to pass through an old hedge line to a stile in a far corner by the road.

4. Climb the steps to the road and turn left along the footway to Tidmington. We pass by Tidmington House and church.

Tidmington House is gabled with a veranda of Tuscan columns from the 18th century. The house originally dates from around 1600 but has been added to over the centuries. The nearby church has fine Norman work and some of the furniture is 600 years old. Look carefully in the churchyard and you will see graves of the musical Beecham family who farmed hereabouts.

A few yards further cross the road to take the lane signed to Tidmington.

The River Stour goes under the road at this point. The bridge belies its age, being from the 18th century with one arch a hundred years older.

5. Walk along the quiet byway to pass Tidmington Farm. Just beyond go through a metal gateway on the right. Take the direction indicated to walk to the stile in the diagonal corner.

6. On a lane turn right. At a junction take the lane left. Past a renovated farm the lane is not surfaced.

7. Some 300 yards past the farm look for a signed bridleway through a metal gate on the right. Follow the way alongside a right hand hedge. Go through a corner metal hunting gate. Keep ahead over the open field. On the far side gradually climb the hill at the border of a left hand hedge.

8. In a corner keep ahead along a track that now climbs steeply through bushes. Over the brow the track becomes a green lane. Drop down to a road and turn right along the B4035 to return to the town.